D0796613

ECHO LIGHT

Echo Light

Kate Gale

RED MOUNTAIN PRESS

Author's photograph by Jamie Clifford, 2013.
Cover image *Four & Twenty* by Giselle Gautreau.

Grateful acknowledgment is made to the following journals in which certain poems in this book first appeared, sometimes under different titles and/or in previous versions: *Eclipse*: "All that Summer Air," "Killing the Almost Jew"; *Gargoyle Magazine*: "Orchard Bees"; *The Georgia Review*: "The Storm Drain"; *Great River Review*: "Grand Canyon"; *Paterson Literary Review*: "Double Journey"; *Poems & Plays*: "Later the Moon Died," "Shura"; *Black Clock* "Echo Light"; *Poetry Flash*: "Every Place Nowhere"; *Rattle*: "Dangerous Blood IV"; *Valparaiso Poetry Review*: "Poker Players."

ISBN 978-0-9855031-8-5
Printed in the United States of America

)⁾\

RED MOUNTAIN PRESS
Santa Fe, New Mexico
www.redmountainpress.us

We were screaming at the edge of the world.
The next lifers called back to us, "Nice music, guys!"

Contents

PART III

PART IV

PART I

Pillar of Cloud by Day, Pillar of Fire by Night

Corn

The floor was full of corn and my breath of silences.
The leaves were gold, red, orange. I wanted blue, but
there were none. My legs were blue where you slapped me,
but we leaned into corn night after night. The arc
of the moon appearing finally, the husks gathered into fire.

The corn husking lasted weeks. My shoulders
bare and whipped along the blades. August burned and blistered.
Corn and sorrow taste salty along the rim of the tongue.
You, coming apart at the seams. The kernels packed on the ears,
milky sweet; when you bit them, they fairly burst.

Roasted with salt they were a direction for life, saltwater, and fire.
I couldn't imagine growing away then. Outside the circle
of firelight was unimaginable blackness. Inside, the rain of blows,
your hands hard and heavy, corn that would give way
to fall apple-picking in the orchard by the stream.

Later I understood that people dream of life by a stream
in a cornfield. What they wished for I could not imagine.
The vultures were there overhead when we husked.
I imagined you would kill me some day. Afterlife would be
an adventure for me, a meal for the vultures, surely.

SNOWSHOES

Who saves the savior?
—Anne Carson

I walked on rocks, forded rivers, my bare heels sliding over stones.
You, mother, never carried me.

Emerged from the other side, a female bear with cubs
I carried across rivers, broke boughs for our nest.

Then it was all feasting. Too much feasting. Too much wine.
Too many times telling the story of the crossing.

The story took on an odd ragged shape, like a child's toy.
Wasn't possible to tell what animal it had been.

What I'm left with in the deathless shade isn't the play between
shadow and story. It's the sound of feet running. Away.

You and I across the moon in snowshoes. Walking carefully
not to break through crust. Branches of trees, ice diamonds.

I was god. My shadow huge and dark. Could flap my wings.
The shadow would scissor and fall into white.

Many years since darkness swallowed me. Disease when shadow
is banished. I walk on snowshoes into bear country where shadows live.

I hear wind rising, snow beginning. Snowshoes make almost no sound.
Up ahead, a house, a thin trail of smoke.

You don't live there; I don't either. I open the door to my witch self
crouched by the fire rubbing hands together. My face too dark to see.

Too young to run away. To old to be worth anything. The in-between part wasted at the races.

But these parts I've got left. When I hold them up, they don't resemble any animal I've seen before.

I hold my face in my lap, not sure whether to burn it or wear it.
In the end it's what I've got: shadow, stories, feathers, eyes.

Don't Appear

Sky isn't everything.
But it is.

Mother shoved my head
under the bench, said,
"Don't appear."

For gladness
I told sky
that it was all.

Sky falling
welcome.
We'd be everything

and so I was.
Appearing.
Where she said,

"Don't."
There
"like the sky" I was.

Visiting Mother

Let us begin with truth clear as glass. I do not.
Cannot. Visit my mother. Where she lives, I cannot go.

I have a picture of her at twenty-three. At sixty-three.
What I am afraid of. Seeing myself.

In those pictures. I am not yet forty-three.
Not yet gone mad.

My daughter at sixteen is like me. Secret biters.
We take a thing with our teeth. Ride down hard.

Until there is nothing left. We hold ourselves separate from men.
Even as we embrace them.

Our bodies outweigh my mother's. Her skin thin as leaves,
her bones like tissue paper, her hair masses of whiteness.

Like windfall snow. All teeth, bones, hair. Our teeth are strong.
We bite back against her absence.

My daughter has seen pictures. Shrugs. Her young, round face holds no regrets.
When I apologize for the missing grandmother she says, *Mother.*

She laughs. It's all old comedy for her. Life is overthehorizon. Not behind.
I watch the 63 year old in the picture as if she might flame to life, grab me by throat.

In the picture, she smiles. My daughter's smile is defiance.
And mine? I search in the mirror, in my hands, it does not come.

Orchard Bees

They compassed me about like bees; they are quenched as the fire of thorns:
for in the name of the Lord I will destroy them.
—Psalms 118:12

The afternoon sun was a rain of bees,
my hair full of wings.
It was the afternoon you left me
in the orchard.

You began to speak Claudius-slow,
then faster as I sat up to listen.
You'd never wanted that second child.
I asked for a drink. The light was clouds.

I couldn't see through air darkening.
Around three, the afternoon filling
with your words. I wanted shade, water.
There was none. You towering over me.

Creating a thin black line across grass.
A falling spear. Nothing like a canopy.
Nothing like shelter. Then the bees began.
Thick afternoon air. Already word-damaged.

I wanted to kill you you said.
Before you were born. While you
were still jellyfish, I wanted you dead.
Still Esau, I wish you dead.

Every day I regret. You spat on the ground;
the bees rose in a swarm and descended
on my round girl's body, new breasts
stomach full of green apples.

My hands stained purple with wildflowers,
my clothes torn, the new shoes you'd bought me
broken down, my whole tangled self
a welter of scratches and bruises.

The bee cloud descended like rain
stinging whispering fighting each other
for a piece of me. They gave their lives
to ruin my pale flesh.

I rose and began to walk, my eyes swollen blood
oozing from my pores my whole body a bruise
I could not speak to you Mother.
Clouds covered the sun; you moved away.

I called to you from swollen lips.
It is finished. I thirst. The afternoon sun
was a rain of bees, and my mouth was full of vinegar
the day you left me in the orchard.

Later, the Moon Died

I'd like to remember it as it really happened. I'd like to remember it. I'd like to remember. It never happened.

A memory. Not a fact. He never tore my. He never tore. He never. He. Never. I can't remember. I'm losing my mind.

There are discrepancies in your story. Discrepancies. A story. Just a story. Only a story. Forget about it. Forget. About. It. What? Now we're talking.

I still remember. Let's go over this again, shall we? Do you or do you not want to see light again? Do you want to eat again? Do you want out of here?

In my life? I'm only ten. Of course I do. I'm only ten. I'm ten years old. You can't imprison me in this room the rest of my life.

Pop goes the weasel. The result is sperm and egg meeting at the Rusty Bar for a drink. The child grows.

You can't imprison me your whole life. My whole life.

I can, and I will. Brick by brick. Layer by layer. I'll brick you in, you little whining, crying Kathy. You'll be in there with the cask forever and ever.

No one will hear your cries.

But you will. You'll hear me.

I won't.

You'll know I'm crying. You'll hear.

I'll keep bricking if it takes my whole life. It's my life's work. It's called growing up.

Call it any name you want. It's murder.

No, murder means you kill a person. You were never a child. Not really a child.
Never properly a child. Shut up. Your face abuses the light. You're a smudge
on the landscape of perfectly formed, deliberate snow drifts.

I've created a snow angel here and here. You're outside the picture.
There's nothing to forget.
You. You little ten-year-old screamer, you never happened.

Shura

It wasn't a face any more. A broken thing.
Opened wide by time, cavernous washes of memory.
Waves of what might have been.
The memory where my sister's face
was is empty of light and shadow.
Time rushed in leaving stains only of itself.
All hollows and blank fields where iridescent sunshine
glances off, goes its own way. Search for eyes shining.
Nothing. Huge dark spaces. Lips that move randomly
around parroted word shapes. A face like leaf shards buried.
What used to be alive pieces floating around
just under the surface, you see them give way to decay.
Used to hold water and sunlight, echo sky even.
Now darkness. A face once. Surely a face.

She shaded her eyes. Said don't come back.
Darkness swallowed the last strands of red.
My skin translucent blue-white, long shadowy scars.
I picture her face still. The first to say goodbye.
The sky west and hung low.

Orchids goodbye stems. Almond trees, goodbye blossoms.
Bright in January. A cloud in the yard. Floating above grass.
Drifting. Then goodbye petals. Another sky just ripples of red,
goodbye sun, the horizon all flame. I clutch sheets at dawn
in disbelief at the sun's rising. In disbelief at you there.

KILLING THE ALMOST JEW

She says, You're almost—not quite—a Jew.
I keep digging. She says, You would have been
had I been Jewish, the mother must be a Jew.
Your father was a neurotic, a Jew.

What's your excuse, Mother? I say.
Just dig. And shut up, once.
I don't harbor neuroses, I say.
I strangle them with my bare hands.

She reaches for me. Hands off my sweet neck.
Your evil neck, half Jew. I dig
'till the hole is large enough to lie down,
let Mother fill it in with a shovel 'till I am buried.

It cheers her every time, killing the almost Jew.
She sings afterward. For a second, when the burial
is complete, I lie still underneath while the dust settles
and hear her, a mad scream of joy, high and clear.

The City

The city where I fell into you
wasn't so much a city as the idea of a city.
You weren't real. You followed me.
I claimed the earth between us. You jumped.

I climbed a thorn tree. You flew.
I had never understood the ring. The token.
I wanted distance between me and the other side
where you see into the hole with no light.

It's a well. One tiny figure at the bottom.
Faults obvious even from your immense height.
You stomping. Clenching and unclenching your hands.
Severed life pieces you couldn't retrieve. Shards.

As a child, they told me if you gnash your teeth at night,
you're guilty. If you dream, you're a liar.
If you fall asleep immediately, it's to hide your sins,
if you sleep in trees, you sleep with the devil.

I fell asleep immediately in trees,
gnashed my teeth and cried.
I had grown. Then it was morning,
and there were no more tears.

Heaven

Squat next to the porch, look under.
Little girl, filthy boy holding hands
secret-like. Light through porch slats.

She says, What do you want?
You say, Nothing, just looking.
She says, we're thinking 'bout music.

Music? About nothing.
The big nothing that happens when you die.
Heaven? you say.

Oh silly, that's just what they say
when you don't act right.
There's no heaven.

I came from there and back last night.
I saw what they call heaven.
What did you see?

Under the porch
it's earth and crabgrass,
bricks for when you're hiding.

It wasn't heaven like they say.
It was big and nothing.
No grownups, just music carrying you.

Joey's still holding her hand.
The sun moves through porch boards,
lines of light on your jeans and sneakers.

The music takes you outrageously close to the sun.
I built a glass castle for us.
We didn't call it heaven.

We called it music.
We lived there
without grown-ups interrupting.

SAVIOR

It isn't true that there was nothing.
That there was no love.
If there was love, I did not find it.
Surely a failure on my part.

It isn't true that I wanted love,
and it did not find me.
I did not know love, would not
have recognized it coming or going.

What I remember.
Great darkness and stars.
The smell of beets steaming, vinegar.
Tomatoes, broccoli, salt.

There was cornbread.
Water to drink. And sleep.
The floor hard, but sleep still.
Entering another world.

I can enter it anywhere, escape.
In cars, riverbanks, offices, planes.
I am cocooned against winter.
Story-safe. Every night I tell me.

Stories. The least of which
is love. My stories are the same story.
Not love. Rescuer, dragon slayer, Joan of Arc.
Not quite. I am, it is true, the hero.

Dangerous as lightning and as fast.
I save myself and one more person from certain death.
The Savior wears sandals, eats fruit,
sleeps on rocks. Is curiously powerful.

We saviors lean over bridges, climb windmills.
Splinters of ourselves go tumbling.
We speak a secret language.
Wind carries our smiles.

The Face of God

A man told me once
under a darkening sky
that my fears, the ones

I breathe like air
Fear breath, low quiet,
stuck in a shell

aren't I a child still? Fear
blooming, blooming into the sweet,
hard blood at my temples

is in direct proportion,
a mathematical equation,
to my distance from God.

I drank my own blue sky,
separated my thought from His.
Not easy. Female thought.

If I suck fear through a straw,
God lies with me in bed whispering commandments
which I crack and crumble.

I beg God to get out of *my* bed.
Find His way past Galilee,
to some distant star where men live.

God could be useful elsewhere
if He tried.
My fear goes with Him.

Mushrooms Growing

Everyone screaming pussy willows
apple blossoms
lilacs opening purple-scented cataracts
heavy-lidded perfume
you said I was a mushroom

In the purpled air, you smashed my face in.
Reached for a rock
missed.
The woods, amplified sound
water over rocks

Your face ablaze,
The angels rejoice to see you disciplined, you said
Do you hear their rejoicing?
I listened.
Here is what I heard.

Water. Trees. Light moving. Mushrooms growing.
Ferns uncurling in the spray of heat. My own heart
beating, in time with the universal clock.
Lips moving. I was tasting years ahead,
years of too much light.

What Love Was

Years ago I asked my mother what love meant.
A slap. Night ringing in my ears. I stopped asking.
Wanted night to go on. Leaves wet. Earth smell rising.

Here in the desert, I found a city where one must fly
around ugly buildings. You stood up and waved your hands.
Indicated a place next to you for a possible landing.

PART II

They were both naked, the man and his wife, and were not ashamed.

The Coroner's Office

Lies and visions.
Blood isn't shed for others.

It runs out onto an unblinking pavement
where rose petals wither.

They'll say he killed her.
Or she died of overwork.

Too much. In the tiny airless room.
An empty crib. The answer. Under a mattress.

She tried to get this child to stay a child.
He moved to Tacoma. Saved trees.

They'll say she died, or he killed her.
Both stories true or false.

Depending on the tilt of the Ferris wheel.
For her, it has always been partway down.

Branches

Branches cross and criss-cross the sky
so many hands trying to wipe it all out.

My wife fears beards, so I grow mine very long
hoping to keep her at bay, her words and longings.

It's easier to beat off than deal with the
talk talk talk. It's easier on both of us.

The blue herons spend the offseason alone,
there is mating season. My husband is a blue heron.

My husband's beard is full of acorns. His eyes of mist.
I can't come into a room without him waving his hands.

At home I talk to him, jungle swift about the day.
I talk in the car; the road sizzles with my words like hot rain.

My father said, Avoid smart women. They rush with ideas.
Shut up. Shut up, I said, remembering the glow of listening.

But some nights in the flat, hot air, I think, Can't we just fuck tonight
without having to dissect globe, community, family?

I say this out loud to the back of my truck.
When I open the door to my house, she's wearing nothing.

She rises slowly like the drift of sea fog.
It all happens so inevitably, but a surprise too.

I hear champagne burst in her hands, the slip
of liquid into glass, and that too is foreplay.

Linen lost is enough language for a night. Cuban dance
music carries me to the center of the room where I do not speak.

We are inside another language, the language of a different country,
syllables slick on my tongue, slipping like overripe fruit.

What We Do During War

Mornings more love. Breakfast then.
Café au lait. Trumpets in the street.
To mark passing soldiers. Geraniums.
Spain marching. Inside breakfast.

Jack's legs around her in the afternoon.
Sunlight washing his loins. She all red hair.
Strawberries by the bed. Cream in and out.
Emily was reserved, he had to break that.

Street full of geraniums.
Lorca's blood spilled out onto the pavement.
The soldier's feet marched by. Emily heard a cry,
thought for a moment it was her own.

English papers would declare Lorca
dragged from his house and killed.
Masses of red geraniums grew over the street.
The sun very bright in Spain.

The Great Divorce

for C.S. Lewis and the fragile women of Los Angeles

You can't talk to me like this.
I told you. Or somebody told you.
Somebody ought to have told you.

I've suffered terribly. I'm fragile.
And therefore. You mustn't. No.
You don't see. I've had to pick myself up.

Hold it all together.
I've been raped by pretty much
every male I've ever met.

A sort of rape anyway.
Something I would characterize as rape.
You can't imagine.

You really have no idea. Don't start.
Let me stop you. Let me pour myself a quick shot
of Hennessy and stop you.

No, I don't want to go to therapy. Don't you see?
This is who I am. That's the problem with most people.
They don't actually see you.

They see it. This thing you hold in front of your face
to keep them out. To keep them from knowing anything
they can hold against you, and they will.

Take Your Blouse Off

In shadow light, your hands reaching.
Let me. Your voice swallows my head.

You said you're fine the way you are.
Take your blouse off. Take it off. It's only streetlight.

I stood there bare-breasted in the road.
Where are you taking me?

You say, Come here. You have leaves
in your hair, grass between your teeth.

Come kiss close. Let me fix you,
girl. Perfect you in no time.

I scream, No. You cannot make me undress
on street corners. I'm not a cutout.

I'm not getting into your car.
I'm the sound you hear leaving.

You say, Christ. Where do you think you're going?
You don't listen. Your ears tuned to you.

You say, Do you know who I am? Or who you are?
I say, No. But we are near the waves. I smell ocean.

Can't hear ourselves. Crashing is all.
Don't know if you're still speaking.

Can't remember what you did wrong.
It's cold, and I need you close.

Saltwater in our hair, our eyes.
White foam against blackness. Your hands all I see.

Joe's Napa Girlfriend

She was drunk and oh-so-pretty.
I had her down on her knees.

I gave her a glass of wine.
I gave her a glass of port.

She licked the rim of the glass.
She licked the rim of *my* glass.

She gave me room in the bed.
She gave me. She gave me.

She liquid and out loud
as if the room were soundproof.

I rush lips and sax loose
under the air. There were no covers.

Her buttocks round as afternoon sunlight
balled up tight and ready to eat.

Her hips handfuls of grace.
Like dreams you reach into.

The leaves across the window. Like sand
spilling into a water glass.

A trickle of fluid light.
Please, I said; the music played on.

Old Monk kept flowing.
She was drunk and oh-so-pretty.

The last time. I found her again.
She was fifty. She was drunk.

SEEING YOU NUDE

It was January cold.
Afternoon sun breaking through.
Still too cold for nudity.
You came by the classroom, said let's go.
You wore jeans, a parka, hat, scarf.

I wore a grey skirt. Our faces white
smudges against the snow landscape.
Sunlight poured gently, light falling
through branches of trees.
You led. I followed to the cabin.

No one was home. The drive unplowed.
Inside the air, raw, an aching cold.
You said, Underneath we're quite different.
I said, Let's see. We piled our clothes neatly.
There we were.

My wing like shoulder blades and yours.
We stood back to back. I was taller.
You were right. To the knees, the same.
Above your knees, hair. Dark places.
White skin unexposed to sunlight.

Its own creature, a wild thing, shy too.
Its head astir, body moving.
None of my body parts anything like it.
We circled each other staring.
Your head cocked.

Like you were examining the Sphinx.
Or an exotic spider. All I could think was,
what are you looking at? I look normal.
No part of my body is rising like a cat
to look around the world.

We left as the light was dying.
You were careful not to touch me all the way back.
I wished for a photograph. A movie.
To show someone. What I could not believe
and would they? It moved.

We come home from Mozart. He pours me brandy. Anxiety on the tongue crawls to anger. The way he walks around the kitchen. At the concert, men had stopped to watch my legs. That was something. He should have appreciated. But failed. A sentence in itself. To see the good in anything. Me or the kid. The one who flunked PE last year. Stayed up 'till midnight. Sucking cellphone waves. Me because. Wives are invisible to their husbands like floating seed pods on a June day. You sense the light mist of them falling. Inconsequential in the summer heat. But new leaves you'd notice. The brandy. Light moving through me. Him. Bathing. Hoping my moon will rise like bubbles, popping, effervescent. I open the window. The cat enters. Is fascinated with itself. When you least expect it. The curtain opens. All that summer air entering and entering, the room swathed in vacant moon heat. There's a moment. Late summer night. Brandy after Mozart. The moth wings of fate moving his way. I want the desire of first night but it's late. I'm not twenty, and the brandy is fine.

Too Drunk

If a man rejoice not in his drinking, he is mad; for in drinking
it's possible . . . to fondle breasts, and to caress well-tended locks,
and there is dancingwithal, and oblivion of woe.
—Euripides, *The Cyclops*

Really? It's not a funny story.
Not even when you tell it.
It's a story. I'll give you that.
You fell from three stories up.
Broke a collarbone. One leg.
She watched. You fell
backwards. Spiraled.
She cried. Over you.
You severed from normal.
She, all edges, became mother, lover.
The collapse of the drunk toward sleep,
aching for the undeliverable.
There's a minute or two,
a glimmer sideways down a long hall.
Fog. Weak winter sunlight.
Light goes out. Small cries.
You were mice. White mice.
She was mice. Chasing you.
Through the maze. No cheese.

CRATER LIGHT

The man drinking whiskey sours tells me about his divorce.
The problem was his wife, apparently. She would not
lie still. Any movement, any distraction caused malfunction.
She knew this. She was warned. Yet she moved arms, ears, toes.

Stay still, he said. His wife underneath.
Said it louder. She froze. The light changed.
Moonlight, shadow. I can't focus, he said.
She opened her eyes. Can I watch?

Better not, he said. Nothing's going to happen.
Stay still. She knew he was right by the way
the moon's craters seized the light, reflected it back
to earth. Unable to create light of their own.

Some receptors create. She was sure of this. She stayed still,
but he was right, nothing happened. What he tells me?
She was warned. He buys me a drink. Hopes my mind will change.
But my mind is with his wife in bed watching the moon's craters.

Corpses Don't Make Love

You can't hear the sun as it rises. You can't know for sure.
As it lifts itself over the mountains toward you. Strung out on wine.
You will be ruined by fifty. Look like seventy.

Feel like eighty. You'll remember wine. An aching.
How you tried for an erection. (He tried for an erection!)
Felt spongy nothing between your legs. (Between your ears.)

Went South. Went to bed. Went to Mexico. Drank more. Withered.
Talked a great deal. When you are eighty. Actually. An erection
may not be possible. (God bless Viagra in its coming and in its going.)

Remember that afternoon in Venice? Lunch. Lobster ravioli.
Back to the hotel room. Quick showers. She, naked in the sliced pear
of afternoon light. On the sheets, rose-pink.

You, drunk and foul, asleep, your body crunched away from her.
When you woke, your breath sour, she, eating raisins by the open window,
wearing a yellow dress. You couldn't speak. Rose to bathe.

You were conscious of being wilted, hairy, grotesquely male in your protrubences.
(If males picture females without clothes, females try not to picture males, the image
too frightening, too obscene.) What you'll know at eighty, corpses don't make love.

You take another drink. You'll drink to that.

Celery Is Good For You

Deep in his spine he understood the day was way too grainy,
his wife's eyes too full. It's better never to send the book out.
Keep it close to the tumbler. With his whiskey he eats celery.
It's healthy. Celery is good for you. This could be a line to start a novel
about an alcoholic. He thinks about this.
Takes another drink. Might as well not leave it.

Unfinished business is nasty. Like the divorce. Like Betsy.
The room half full of street light. Half full of shadows.
Pickup truck in the driveway. Lately it's hard remembering.
He's not sure where he left the shovel. The glass of liquid startles him.
Movement and life. Almost a life of its own.
Almost staring back at him. Almost speaking.

The Mouth Under the Mango Tree

The tree over them darkness gathering
he found her lips first skirts light
mouth wet open let's stop here
she's nearly fifteen nearly ready for marriage
I'm not ready for children
I won't tell her there's anything else
her mouth her mouth
opening in the dark
above them the mango tree dripping

STREWN SHEETS, HOP JUICE

At first soap. Just washing.
Then hopped-up juice.
Then sloppy kisses.
Breasts aching like leaky boats.
Stomach full of fear.

Mornings smell of figs, ripe cherries.
I say, Joe. He says, Impossible.
We only lie about naked.
Drink hop juice.
Play organ music.

Nights blow dust.
Joe, this is now.
We eat cucumbers, lentils, flat bread.
Joe's Dad works around to cheese.
I move to Joe's bedroom 'till the baby.

The whole country is full of light.
Joe dreams we're married.
I squeeze lemons onto couscous.
At the center of the table, lilies.
In the mirror my hair is blue.

An accident. But maybe.
If we can tell stories
to each other. Leftover
words are what we have
mostly. That and staring at blue.

Grand Canyon

We ate oysters, habañero sauce. You had fish
wrapped in banana leaves. The orange sky
lifted the room. The table seemed large.
As if I couldn't pass things to you. As if
your words would never make it to me.

You said, he and I are no longer us.
You said we kiss goodnight, but it doesn't mean anything.
When he first fell for me, we dressed in drag every day.
You said there's no point in bows or heels or sequins.
Wigs are pointless without Jim.

I showed you the Grand Canyon spread out.
I said it's a large void, no doubt.
Could a car make it without falling in,
from the North Rim to the South Rim?
On the map, it looks very close.

Maps lead you to believe strange things. Maps an illusion.
Distance is as you live. You said what's the space between rims?
It's children, money, relatives, alcohol, weed, madness.
It's Vivienne locked away, so Tom wouldn't have to hide from her.
Eliot coolly collecting his prizes. There's your Grand Canyon.

You said, from the helicopter, I see Jim's back and shoulders.
The canyon open, pink inside with river at the bottom. It's a gash
in the landscape. Not at all, it's an opening into another world.
Hike down through it. There are shells in the strata.
Donkeys, people, water, incredibly slanted light.

PART III

Don't ever ask for the true story.
—Margaret Atwood

Savior with a Pipe

He sat there smoking all day. Smoking his pipe. A donkey would walk by. He wouldn't notice. Just stare at the sky. Ask himself questions like, Will it rain? He had saved the world many times in his bed. He'd saved every woman from dying in her bed. His own women left him one by one. Sneaked off to motels in the middle of the night. Learned to speak Spanish. Fled the country. None of this would have ever happened if there hadn't been so much to do. He collected ceramic cars. Smoked his pipe. None of his four children ever called. He threw cherry pits to the pigeons who hopped after them on city streets. His daughter hanged herself in Tucson. His life tide contained things not people. In the crowd passing, he sensed a familiar gait. An ex-lover? Son? Grandson? Didn't matter.

Dangerous Blood IV

It didn't take even a drink to wet open her.
Untie her face so words stepped in.

Talc all over the floor of Grandmother's kitchen.
It's what her grandmother wore to bed.

Grandpa loved it. You mixed flour, salt,
baking powder, made biscuits.

Then tea. While they were hot,
buttery the unlacing began.

Usually she preferred women
who would not bruise open her.

Men. Clumsy hands. Grunts. A face looming
over hers twisted into an indecent mask of pleasure.

The face heavy-lidded almost angry
with ecstasy. She wanted safe.

Her girls weren't boot-laced, all teeth and appendages,
leathered like the smart things in bars.

Hers were fresh open, limp-legged.
Now she, astride this male, had to answer

his groans with her own, bite back.
She tore along his belly like she never

dared to tear the fevered females in dark on satin.
Out loud she screamed. Certainly the curtains were open.

The scream carried along on the night winds. Badgers
in their dens snuffled approval, animal sounds at night.

Leaf Triangle

It's what you find down there. If you dare.
Or so I hear in serious parts of town.

When I was growing up, sex wasn't mentioned.
Like croutons. Just there. Part of the salad. Flavor.

Don't lick the knife, they said. Lick spoons. And we did.
Lick frosting, cookie dough. Off spoons.

I asked where the center of the universe was.
Different answers. The forest where acorns scatter the floor.

A volcano. The smelting place where stars are born. Getting enough sleep,
one old broad laughed. Being woken up, said another.

One girl, hair like leaf mold, older than me, so old, probably nineteen,
hands already calloused, fair skin like the open palm of the sky told me,

Leaf Triangle. She smiled, like it was a big secret,
like it would take me forever to understand.

THE LAST SKIRTS OF DAY

The way he licked her ear.
That mattered. Tongue warm.
Her hair a wet-tangle. Nattered grey silk.
She could feel his tongue and not move.
July Paris. Hot breath of streets.
The head seemed to hold still then fall.
Crowd noise. Hand under her blouse.
She cocked her head. Rain soon. Surely rain.
The day gathered its skirts.
Crowd slowed. Wind died.
He reached for her hand; she was tired
of everything. He had taken too long to get there.
She was ready to go home for wine and fruit.
Even bread. The day sighed and went out.

Radishes

Hammock girlfriends plan diet.
Blouses open. Summer light.
Radishes by the plateful.
Dandelion greens okay too.
Tame on wild. Blouses open.
You never need to go hungry again.
Radishes not enough
You know. Come to me.

Living with Ghosts

The boy wasn't listening.
The house was dangerous.
You can't get away from the house
you're born with.

They don't want the boy to grow.
Feel under skirts on the train.
Can't the boy grow up to be a poet?
There is no way out. What story do you want?

Smudges of stories against brightness.
Ghosts holding them like thread.
The house incredibly damaged.
The boy within. That blue light, not skirts.

What if later he escapes haunting? Hears the click.
Gets outside the damaged mind. Sees blue.

Los Angeles

I have known the arms already, known them all—
Arms that are braceleted and white and bare . . .
—T.S. Eliot

Los Angeles people look right through you,
see little ghosts with no shape or color.

Money gives a body form like a straitjacket
holding you against wind, pestilence.

You are shadow against dusk. Cream against pale.
All colors not cream become sunshine.

I have stood in the sill of time counting my days, the cups full of cries
and laughter, paint and words, silence and tea equal nothing here.

Los Angeles, once a desert glitters green.
The green holds you up against sky. Gives you shadow.

That shadow casts longing across beaches and highways.
As morning opens, you see hands stretching out for a piece.

The palm trees are restless. Your silhouette an outline.
Light streams across you, you are nothing.

You must be thin to cast a shadow. You must
drive a cool car. You must have blond highlights.

There is no place for silence. I stare in the mirror. Cover face with hands.
My hands hold my reflection. In the mirror I see nothing.

Poker Players

Poker players eat corn relish on hotdogs.
Sing out of key. Hum classic rock.
Tangential conversations stop, start.
Rooms full of chair-scraping.

The devil sat down to play poker opposite
the blue-eyed woman in grey. She said, I bet
my husband's sink. Not my own. I need it
to wash my face and hands.

The poker players drank smoke, smelled
of shoe leather. The ache and fever of the game,
the rain mixed with the devil's whistle. The voice
of God never reached her. She knew better

than to get up from her chair. The clock struck five.
The ceiling glowed red. She held up her cards.
A good hand. Smiled. The devil laughed,
all teeth and wild hair.

She held her cards like her husband's face.
Both were her winnings.
Hers to lay down. Hers to pick up.

Protestors at the Federal Building

Figures against traffic in the setting sun.
To continue disturbance long after they are dead.
Clouds reef up sails westward over the ocean.

The protestors on Wilshire hold candles
against city traffic. Weeping for the babes
of Bethlehem. Asking someone in charge to stop.

But the someones are too far away to hear.
Too high above the streets to smell sweat.
A protestor will be arrested for obstructing traffic.

An ex-priest stands among them, his hands raised in blessing.
The protestors in the shadow of Wilshire buildings
object to the rain of fire and brimstone on humans.

Cars pound by like bulls on their way to slaughter.
The ex-priest will bless them in their coming
and in their going. He will bless us all.

Sailor

Everything depends on the lilt
of your slow movements. Well-water deep.
In rooms full of people, you hold yourself
in a bottle. Women feel comfortable
with you. Not you with them.

Darkness swallows your last shadow. Shadows, helpless,
beautiful, thriving in moonlight, sinking like wings
as light sinks. Your shadow exists somewhere to rise
when you wake, heave itself about the room
smelling of roses and ripe figs.

If you're not careful, Sailor, you'll be alone
in that room. The ripe figs all. No fragrance
rising like odors of clams and mussels
to grab you by the hair, push you down
into the throat of sea water past hunger.

Into the stupor at the center of the world
where dreams emerge, where fragrance
is a newborn child and "I am" breathes
in the subterranean floods we once waited for,
erupting out of the earth like the breath of gods.

The Red Cap

Water hurries down the street
flat, grey, drainage humming.
The sky heavy on the land.
California undone by water.
Street isn't everything.

I run past houses closed up.
Dogs barking. School children
not saying lessons. Staring out.
Dreaming of a world where kids/ducks interchange.
Ducks go to school. Waddle forward to the board.

Gretchen walks out the house. Slippers.
Eyes me. With one frisbee motion
flings the red cap onto the street.
Lands head up, water immediately.
A car runs over Doug's red cap.

Gretchen's back inside. Coffee cup.
Newspaper. Weather and world changing.
Her life too. Why not? Throw out the trash.
Some's recyclable. Some not.
I run still. The rain heavy now.

Past the trash truck. Leftover garage sale items.
Books on Christ. For sale.
A scooter. Ninety dollars brand new. Nine now.
Like my knees. Going to hell fast.
I run for fear of fat. Age. Not being able to run.

Fear of being left behind. Just you
coming back. Pity or guilt shaking you.
Almost home now. I check out Doug's cap.
Flattened. Part of the street nearly.
Doug's head absent.

RUSSIAN BLUE

Small motel room. Thin carpeting, bedding.
Picture of a wolf on the wall. A woman naked.
Bathtub filling. Bathroom full of yellow light.
Her veins dark in the crook. She misses her cat.

Between rehab and halfway house is a leap.
Turns on the TV. Blue light. Beautiful people.
A thin, naked man had taken her in huge thrusting moments
enjoying her available ecstasy. Just bring home the dope, I'm yours.

She was queen of the block. Uniquely thin in the fat part of the Valley.
She'd been his, kitten-cute. He left when he noticed ants, flies, smell,
long un-bathed summers, diapers, unfed dog, cat with no litter box,
broken mirror, ashtrays floating in the sink.

She spread out thin veiny arms, came into the driveway naked.
He shoved her backward. She fell like a palm swaying backward in sea air.
The tub full and overflowing. She calls her cat on the phone,
turns on the TV louder, says her prayers, drinks her whiskey straight.

The last thing is the cat, a huge Russian Blue. If only she had the cat.
She calls out, "Smokey," she can't remember if it is still alive or if she is.

SAM, BEFORE THIS DONKEY

Wretched underwear. Coffee. Thirty-eight. Realizing women find all this fixable,
cute even in a twenty-something, irresistible in their teens, revolting at forty. Hairy.
Should shave. Not that it would change the way women's eyes drift around him,
avoiding him. Offended even. It's raining again.

He's tired of looking around the eyes. Nobody can *feel* yellow says his therapist.
The last woman was common. Left the shower stall ajar when she bathed.
Found him unnecessary. Met Clyde who could really party.
No match for Clyde's coke connections, he's back to flipping channels.

At night, frozen food or restaurants. Learning to cook would be admitting defeat.
Drives home, spots a donkey, eyes closed in his driveway. Rides the donkey
up the little hill in his backyard. The sun darkens. Gets off the donkey.
Leans into a tree. Tries to remember the redhead's name.

It's hot July. Thinks of icicles dripping. From eaves. Used for swordplay once.
Back then. A boy wielding his icicle. Being swordplay. Before this donkey.

Early Writers

When writing on parchment began, he was saddened
to step away from the cave wall.

He'd started writing and drawing as a spelunker.
Liked exploring the dark echo space.

Water tapping far off. His helper Gregory
with such lovely legs, holding the candle.

Gregory's huge, dark-lashed eyes
opening in the cave darkness.

He drew in red ochre to wake the dead,
remind the living we were warriors.

Parchment meant sitting indoors. He wanted
to garden, go for a walk, visit his niece Josefina.

Josefina, Gregory, the starlings, the garden,
his own masterful cooking, the way light moved

all too webbed into his frame to withdraw
to his room to write.

He began drawing trees into margins
went outside to study them, blue foxgloves.

Willows laced letters, leaves trailing through.
He made parchment come alive.

Gregory sang to him while he wrote; some days he'd
hear the rain in the corn, miss the caves.

He and Gregory would tramp out at dawn
find red markings on the cave wall.

The battles, love, the first man kissing
the first woman.

God looking exactly like them, creating
foxgloves, blue petals in his fingers glowing.

One Good Eye

The lonely woman has ten fingers, one good eye. She asks for a basket for her
journey filled with sandwiches. Is given a basket sprinkled with salt containing
one snake. Old, dry, shriveled. Crawls in her lap. Offers to share the journey.
She buys bread, mangos, wine. The snake shares all.

The lonely woman sees the cutter's son, all dark hair and smashing eyes.
Does not speak to her. Stares at instructions for opening the window.
His father predicted an emergency stop. The woman drinks her wine, eats
her bread. The sun sets. Sees her hair has more grey than she'd thought.

She is part woman now, part thing. Shadow against wall.
Cloud against sky. The "part thing" men fear. In the streets,
no one sees the lonely woman. Perhaps there is nothing to see.
Perhaps there is no woman. Only thing. Men and their shadows.

PART IV

You could not believe I was more than your echo.
—Margaret Atwood

Language This

Already too crowded the party
music hipping hopping
underneath underwear
under there human fur
sing party

you touched the man's hand
out night cigarettes weed
you inside a word
with no meaning
language this

I needed him he needed me
we him he inside me inside
my throat open his hands
flute music coming
language this

later he needed her
they outside filmy glass
figures thrown back
me inside outside
language this

me top the house
blackened sky once fresh
it began at a party
upstairs you my throat
language this

Outside the Womb

She opens the door into chaos
limbs sprawled in unimaginable intimacy.
Drowsy in the late afternoon sun.
Light caked, iced on their figures.
The room lopsided with clothing.
A shoe on the nightstand.
One overturned wine glass.
Her stepfather's head thrown back.
She takes it all in, steals a cigarette.
The whole room is padded with light particles.
She remembers her mother's damaged voice,
face blurry with tears.

She wants. She wants.
The sky doesn't remind her of anything.
It is blue everlasting, full of crows.
Leaves falling, asking nothing.
She'll raid the whiskey tonight, crawl to bed.
There's something in her father's tight fist
that she wants to remember. The shape of his head
as he left. The square of his shoulders. The silence
in the house is unbearable. She turns on the TV.
Hoping to smudge out those collapsed figures
prone as gods, drawing golden breath,
possessing what she never will.

From where their bodies lie, she feels
a furnace of happiness. Beside that, her own life
seems blue, incredibly light as if like the sky
it had no beginning, no ending. This is solid,
the work of the threads through the quilt,

the shape of their feet along the covers,
her mother's air fanned out, and his arms
curved around her mother's head like a swan's
neck bending and swooping in reflected pond light.
Perhaps this moment has no beginning, no ending.
They have always been there, she has always been
perched on the sidelines, watching.

The Clocks Are Winding Down

I went to her house after too much drink. Drank in the fire, party, Jacuzzi.
Men pouring drinks. Boys, men, drummers.
For me it was all party. For her, the noise clouded the clocks.
The endless clocks striking midnight all over the world.

Cringing at too much light.
Crumpled silk in drawers, an old pistol,
a joke. As if there were intruders. As if.
Her father's picture on the wall. Young still.

Always a light on. When I arrived
with the boys in the band, a party. Liquor.
In bright long bottles with strange names.
We mixed concoctions that made us spit up.

Evenings. I'd arrive, sawdust heels from a college bar.
A record signed, "This face seats five." And the band.
She was ready. Music. Big hair. Lipstick.
Smiles that could polish your teeth.

She had the house. We were the party.
Mornings, we left her to dreams of the streetcar
that brought her here. Her prince.
Boys who came out at night.

Our playthings were days, weeks, hours.
The future unmapped, hazy as a country
over a horizon full of dense fog. So busy
were we with Bacchus, dreams did not become us.

She was dreaming backward. Of a future if . . .
If boys had not become men with monsters in them.
Unable to carry her through thorny adulthood.
She, left with photographs, a trunk of tinsel,

looks that faded in sunlight, the taste of bourbon.
We were the window behind her. To the
white pillared beauty of her girlhood before the gods
spanked reality into her bones leaving her speechless.

When last I saw her, the lines were covered with paint.
Her breasts round, her face a mask. She was waiting still,
may be there now for all I know. I wanted to speak to her,
but I was outside her country, couldn't speak the language.

DRUMMING IN THE CRACKS OF GOD

He painted my portrait ugly. All around me in studio lovely men,
shadowy shoulders, creamy flanks, cock glow. Sprouts from purpled deep,
tender stamens' pollen drip of hazy butter-land.

Stravinsky cracks sound like God beats. Early performances people walk out shaking.
What's this? Light opens shutters wide to moon surprise. I hear drumming.
Nothing today. My eyes open for cracks in the face. That place in the earth open.

EVERY PLACE, NOWHERE

Here are needles laid out for some
vast and curious purpose. Quiet.
Later music shaking up the curtains.
Filthy talk, Grandma would say. Sluts.

It's a party, a shakedown rumble.
The smoke alive and drifting. Skirts.
Panties, thongs, boxers, bra straps,
tattoos, tongues, thighs all. Showing.

This is brief happiness. Or what passes
these days for fun. Or what passes. These days.
In an unquiet world where the self is blurry
against the backdrop. Of things.

It's things that define us. And places
we've been. The tile in our houses. Counter tops.
Trips we've taken. To parts of Europe
where you haven't been. But we have.

Conversations empty as air after broom passes
through, crushing back nonsense. Empty.
What we don't talk about. Loneliness.
Our time alone. Ourselves alone. Nobody.

This time. Quiet as shadows. Not even my lover.
Just my secret self against nothing. Breathing.
Speaking elephant language. No one to translate.
Words would float until leaf caught. Then vanish.

Instead of the Committee on Fact-Based Hieroglyphs

You can spend your life around boats, or you can sail away.

You were doing great work./I know.
Why quit? The meetings/It was time.
We want you back./It's over.
Everyone misses you/If I were dead.
We just want to know./Nothing to say.
Why you walked off./My story?

Because the committee does important work.
In the field of hieroglyphs.
Because I was the head of the committee.
Because I traveled to Tehran the year of the sand storm,
literally picked sand fleas off
camels belonging to the organization.

Because I'd forgotten how to write.
Because I'd forgotten how light pours into Evolution Valley
until the bears stop eating to watch that light.
The light that asks for pen, colors, a canvas.
Those teenagers cracking the world's oldest jokes.
Your face when the valley opens up, your beard dripping.

Sleep

Me, I was part of the nastiness now . . . But the old man . . .
in a little while . . . would be sleeping the big sleep.
—Raymond Chandler

She said, I'll be laid up a month or so.
She said, they're taking a piece of me the 14th.
She said, please wait a week to see me.

Her voice with all of her intact sounded fragmented.
I said, what if you need something?
She said, I'll lay out the world for myself.

From operating table to home studio with whiskey,
water, and a straw. She said I'll chew lemongrass,
that's for healing, drink green tea, that's for prayer.

She said, I've been wanting sleep for ages.
I thought of this operation, the chaos in my cells,
then painfully and gloriously, of all that sleep.

Suppertime

Biscuits. Soup. Pepper on soup.
Your father says shut up.
I am with you 'till the end of the world.

You're at the kitchen table.
The family netted in the ferocious skeins
that kill dolphins, a triangle of love and hatred.

Love that drains blood from the corpse afterward.
I'm with you 'till the end of the world.
I will never leave you or forsake you.

Just leave for once. For once in our life.
The music plays on giddy as movie romances.
The family dinner cold. What's left.

The net hugs leeches, eels, birds, all together.
Untangle my fingers. Give me slices of air. Of pomegranates.
This blight cannot be the last feast. Outside are apples.

Feed me apples. Wash me. Let me walk through the gate,
As if I were alone and had invented the world
and was there to name my own kith and kind.

What Judy Said

To say I rarely plan would be untrue. I'm all about plans.
I plan to change the world. Shift the planetary axis just a little. I start at home.

I plan to turn myself into an hourglass, a cloud-shaped woman, a woman-
shaped cloud, a good-looking cloud, not one of those cumulonimbus numbers.

All grey and rain. A woman for whom tears are sawdust. A woman
who has nothing to cry about. Nothing to be ashamed of either.

What I'm afraid is if there's nothing to cry about or be ashamed of, there may be
nothing to sing about. Singing and crying aren't the same thing. But close.

What Judy said to me in the booth by the sea, "Your fingers will travel where they
should not. You travel without a compass."

She said, "You lack substance." Didn't say what substance. The American
woman is too familiar. I did not want to be an American woman.

Had traveling fingers. Wasn't an hourglass. Found Jesus. Then lost him.
There's the truth, and there's what Judy said.

My fingers haven't traveled enough. In the place you coveted,
where juice landed is an island of crows' feet. My fingers traveled.

What plans should I make? Live astride the universe in my green cords?
Let's dream into spaces between stars, let's plan large, let's do what Judy said.

The Storm Drain

Liquid canopy descending sky.
It's dark inside the storm drain but you took me here.
Tongue slow lips open hands lightly under.

When I'm eighty no one will crawl with me
in a storm drain to hold my breasts
while the sky is falling.

I lean into corrugated metal. Rust.
Age. Wet. My back into all that.

Night Howl

God said, Let there be light
and there was light.

Light moved across her belly
and thighs and between.

God spoke and opened the fountains
of the deep. There was water everywhere.

On the sheets and in the bed. And the evening
and the morning were the third day.

Mexican Light

Went to Mexico. Curved sweet tequila light. Lay on blankets on the beach, washed our mouths in morning. Ate olives with sunshine. Avocados. Street vendors sold popsicles. If someone had a hotel room, we all showered. Our spectacular young bodies curved under water. Our breasts moons. The room was white stone. We would start with beer in the afternoon. Hit the cantinas in the evening. My friend would find weed, and Lily would breathlessly come back to my table and say, Katie, I've found you a dyke, the cutest one in Mexico. We would begin shots, chased with lime, tomato juice, the whole evening a tremulous tequila bubble. They played our rock music in Spanish. My boy would dance with me, while Lily and I kissed the girls one right after another. Mexico was like that. When I arrived blue, I would find a blue world. Time moved the craziest of clocks. Stretched on sand we waited for the end of loneliness. Night flies, gulls and beyond them the sea. The sea spoke low sweet Spanish we could almost understand. That was when I noticed what I liked best about you was that you kissed like a girl, looked at me like a girl, danced like a girl; the mescal was thick and smoky, your thin arms came up around me as the sun rose. You said, I'll be whatever you want me to be.

Liebersong for Clouds

Clouds face the earth spread out flat for miles
then ridges. Mountains could bring you to tears.

Walls, faces. Hurried roads. Clouds join with owls.
Feathered wet blackness. Night crowds threaded with clouds.

When clouds sink into towns, it breaks them,
the hard rushing, fine brittle lines of energy raking people.

All that held anger between people.
The clouds break into trees, rooftops staring back.

There are no tears like those for the walking dead.
In our cells we are water.

If we eat it, if we let it come to us.
If we ask it out for the night.

Echo Light

What Helen of Troy and the cheerleaders
know is that there were myths
they almost believed.

I'm sorry, but you aren't. You aren't.
The shadows are your skirts. The space
between your eyes where light does not fall.

Your mouth fails to gather or connect happiness.
Your face moves down hallways like a piece of string.
When were you a solid object? Long ago.

They had fights over you. You believed myths
about the way light falls, spins, bundles.
That light would curve over your shoulders forever.

At any time you could have loosened
the shadows from your hair like a scarf in wind.
You could have, but you did not.

You ate clouds of silence,
breath of breath, blood of your blood,
the sound of your skin, shadows, grief.

Double Journey

A double journey, conscious seeing.
Open-faced dreaming.
The sky undressed to the ankles.
Down came hair, blouse, skirt.
In pictures, I look like a round apple.

Are you a part-time waitress?
I'm not part-time anything.
Everything I do is full-time.
Mostly, I'm a full-time flounder.
Floundering through my life.

It was all a rage of white-washed memory.
It was all a lie. The light fading.
There are no trees in the house.
We put them in the backyard.
The outside creeps them out, the trees.

The trees would like the sky
to themselves, their phallic tips
into all that blue-white cloudscape.
If you have your way with the sky,
the orgasm is enormous.

It was all open-faced dreaming. In pictures
I looked like a nomad with a round belly.
Brown face and legs, everything else pale.
There's blue rising and underneath a round table.
The pillars no longer hold up the sky.

It must float unfastened from the air.
The round table seats eight who came down
from the boat with camels. Why not just sky?
There are no birds. Only cockroaches. Chickens.
The last table. The last sky.

This book is set in Adobe Jenson, designed by Robert
Slimbach. The Roman design is based on the oldstyle face
cut by Nicholas Jenson in 1470, and its italics are based
on those designed by Lusovico Vicentino degli Arrighi.
Book design and composition by Mark E. Cull.